The Try Not To

Laugh Challenge

Easter Edition

How To Play

Step 1

Split into two teams whether that be boys vs girls, kids vs parents, or any mix of your choice. If possible, also assign one person as a referee. You can also do 1 vs 1!

Step 2

Decide who gets to go first. Which team can do the most pushups? Which team can guess the number between 1 and 10 from someone not playing the game? Or just a good old fashioned rock paper scissors?

Step 3

The starting team has to tell a joke from the book. You can say the joke however you like and animate it too with funny faces, gestures, voices or whatever else!

Step 4

If everyone on the opposing team laughs, the other team gets a point! Set a limit for how many points it takes to win and the first team to reach the limit, wins!

What made the Easter Bunny cross the road?

The chicken took his eggs!

What's the Easter Bunny's favorite dance move?

The Bunny Hop

What did the Easter Bunny think of the activities?

He said they were eggcellent!

Why should you be careful when telling Easter Eggs jokes?

Because they might crack up!

What's the Easter Bunny's favorite type of jewelry?

14 carrot gold

What's the Easter Bunny's favorite restaurant?

IHOP!

What's the cross between a bee and a bunny?

A honey bunny

Which kind of bows can't be tied?

Rainbows

What's the best way to send mail during Eater?

Hare mail

How does the Easter Bunny dry his fur?

Using a hare dryer!

How is Easter concluded?

With an r

What's a rabbit with the sniffles called?

A runny bunny

How is the Easter Bunny able to paint all those eggs?

By hiring Santa's elves during their off season!

What's the cross between a rabbit and an insect?

Bugs Bunny

What is a bunny with a big brain called?

Egg head

What makes the Easter Bunny's fur so smooth?

Using his hare brush

What did the candy say to the chocolate on Easter?

You're sweet!

How is the Easter Bunny able to keep his fur so shiny?

By using hare spray

What's an Easter Egg's least favorite day?

Fry day

What did the bunny say to the carrot he was eating?

Been nice gnawing you!

Where does Christmas come before Easter?

In the dictionary!

How can you make Easter easier?

By changing the 't' with an 'i'

What makes the Easter Bunny and Michael Jordan similar?

Both of them are great at stuffing baskets!

What bunny can't hop?

One made of chocolate!

What's the cross between the Easter Bunny and a very famous general in history?

Napoleon Bunnyparte

Easter Bunny's favorite sport?

Basketball

Who is every bunny's favorite actor?

Rabbit De Niro

What happened to the egg when it was tickled?

It cracked up!

What happened to the Easter Bunny when he was in school?

He was egg-spelled due to misbehavior!

Which sport do eggs excel at?

Running

What did one Easter Egg say to the other during recess?

Heard any good yolks recently?

When does Valentine's Day come after Easter?

In the dictionary

Which state capital does the Easter Bunny like the most?

Albunny, New York

What do you call a bunny that knows how to tell a good joke?

A funny bunny

What did the Irishman say on Easter?

AYEEERISH you a Happy Easter!

Where did the rabbits go after their wedding?

On a bunnymoon

What's a rabbit with fleas called?

Bugs Bunny

What's another name for a forgetful bunny?

A hare brain

What's the Easter Bunny's favorite method of travel?

Hare plane

Where does the Easter Bunny get his eggs from?

An egg plant

What is yellow with long ears and grows on a tree?

The Easter Bunana

Difference between a crazy bunny and a counterfeit bill?

One's a mad bunny and the other is bad money!

How come everyone is always so tired in April?

Because they just finished getting through a March!

What put the Easter Bunny in such a bad mood?

Having a bad hare day!

What's a rabbit working in a bakery called?

The Yeaster Bunny

What happens when you leave a chocolate bunny outside in the sun?

You get a runny bunny!

How are you able to find out if the Easter Bunny has been somewhere?

Because eggs mark the spot!

What's a rabbit with a dictionary in his pants called?

A smarty pants

How does the Easter Bunny like to stay in shape?

By doing hare-obics!

What's big, purple and likes to hug your Easter Basket?

The Easter Barney

Why was the bunny wincing her eyes?

Because she had an eggache!

What do bunnies put on their booboos?

An eggaid

Why was the father egg always so strict?

Because he was hard boiled!

What should you say to others on Easter if jumping around?

Hoppy Easter!

What do you call an egg that is being mischievous?

A practical yolker

What's a fatigued Easter Egg called?

Eggzausted

What happened to the lady whose home became infested with Easter Eggs?

She had to call the eggsterminator!

Why did the Easter Bunny go to jail?

For hare-assment

What kind of beans does the Easter Bunny grow at home?

Jelly beans

What kind of music does the Easter Bunny mostly listen to?

Hip hop

Why did the Easter Bunny go into hiding?

Because he was a little chicken!

What's long, colorful and shows up only once per year?

The Easter Parade!

How come the Easter Egg didn't cross the road?

Because he wasn't a chicken yet!

What should you do if your Easter Eggs disappear?

Demand an eggsplanation!

What did the mother egg say to her baby egg?

You're eggstra special to me!

How long does the Easter Bunny like to party?

Around the cluck!

What store do you recommend going to if you lose your tail?

Why the re-tail store of course!

What's the name for multiple rabbits walking backwards?

A receding hare line

What do you call a small bunnythat collects cans?

A wee-cycler

What made the woman sad after the race?

The fact that an egg beater!

Have you heard the story of when the hare sat on the bee?

That one's a tender tail!

What is the Easter Bunny's favorite story?

Anything with a hoppy ending!

Why are you studying your Easter candy?

I'm trying to decide what came first... the chocolate chicken or the chocolate egg?

Easter Bunny's favorite story?

A Cotton Tail

What's the cross between a rabbit's foot and poison ivy?

A rash of good luck

What is an egg from space called?

An egg-straterrestrial

What makes bunnies the luckiest animals?

The fact that they have 4 rabbit's feet!

Don't make fun of the Easter Bunny or else...

He'll get hoppin' mad!

What happened after the Easter Bunny met the love of his life?

They lived hoppily ever after!

How can you prove that carrots are good for the eyes?

Well have you ever seen a bunny wearing glasses?

What kind of stories does the Easter Bunny like the most?

The ones with hoppy endings!

What's the problem with Easter jokes?

They tend to crack you up!

What was the result of the bunny getting his head stuck in the fan?

He took ears off his life!

Why are Easter Eggs so scared of going out in the morning?

They don't want to get scrambled!

What do all the Easter Bunny's friends say about him?

That he's egg-ocentric!

What's red, blue and makes the Easter basket soggy?

Colored scrambled eggs

How come a rabbit's foot cannot be 12 inches?

Because then it's a rabbit's foot!

What's a trumpet player's favorite time of the year?

March

Why couldn't the Easter Egg's family watch cable?

Because their TV was scrambled!

Why was the Easter Bunny hopping down the road?

He was filming a movie!

Enjoying the book? Let us know what you think by leaving a review!

What has your favorite joke been till now?

What's the Easter Bunny's reward for making a basket?

Either 2 or 3 points

What's the cross between the Easter Bunny and a crazy person?

An Easter basket case

What's Ireland's version of James Bond?

Dublin 07

Difference between a bunny and lumberjack?

One hews and chops while the other chews and hops!

How many Easter Eggs can you put in an empty basket?

One! Because after that, it's not empty anymore.

Cross between the Easter Bunny and Chinese food?

Hop suey

Where does the Easter Bunny study medicine?

At John Hopkins

Why do we paint Easter Eggs?

Because that is much easier than putting wallpaper on them!

How come the Easter Bunny threw his watch during the party?

Apparently, time flies when you're having a blast!

What's the result of pouring hot water down a rabbit hole?

Hot cross bunnies

Knock Knock

Who's there?

Harvey

Harvey who?

Harvey good Easter everyone!

Knock knock

Who's there?

Anne

Anne who?

Anne-other Easter Bunny!

Knock knock

Who's there?

Police

Police who?

Police hurry up and decorate your eggs!

Knock, knock.

Who's there?

Don.

Don who?

Don be puttin' down Easter.

Knock, Knock

Who's there?

Warren

Warren who?

Warren anything colorful today?

Knock, knock.

Who's there?

Boy.

Boy who?

Boy do I love Easter!

Knock Knock

Who's there?

Howard

Howard who?

Howard you like a chocolate bunny?

Knock Knock

Who's there?

Arthur

Arthur who?

Arthur any more Easter eggs to decorate?

If you enjoyed the book, be

sure to check out our other fun

books as well by searching

"<u>Hayden Fox</u>" on Amazon!

As a special bonus, enjoy this

exclusive preview of one of our best-

selling titles!

Would You Rather

Book for Kids

A Hilariously Fun Activity Book

for the Entire Family

GAME RULES:

Step 1

Make two teams. It can be 1v1, parents vs kids, older kids vs younger kids, girls vs boys or whatever else you like. Pick one referee if possible.

Step 2

Decide who's going to go first. Try a pushup or situp contest? A who can hold their breath for the longest contest? Which team can guess the number between 1 and 10 from the referee? Which team has the youngest player? Or just some good old fashioned rock paper scissors?

Step 3

The starting team has to ask a question from the book and the opposing team has 10 seconds to not only choose an option but to also give a reason for their choice.

Step 4

The team can discuss their answer together but only one player can say the answer and reason out loud. The person answering has to alternate every turn thus the same person from the team cannot answer the next turn The referee decides whether the answer is acceptable.

Step 5

If the player who is answering can't choose or give a good reason then that player is out for the game and can't answer anymore or be involved in the team discussion.

Step 6

Repeat until all players are eliminated.

Would you rather...

*Be a superhero **OR** a wizard?*

Would you rather...

*Have the ability to fly **OR** read minds?*

Would you rather...

*Lick the floor **OR** lick someone's armpit?*

Would you rather...

*Be a cat **OR** a dog?*

Would you rather...

*Fall into a puddle of mud **OR** into a pile of yellow snow?*

Would you rather...

*Do 100 pushups **OR** 100 situps?*

Would you rather...

*Get yelled at by Mom **OR** Dad?*

Would you rather...

*Run 10 miles **OR** bike 50 miles?*

Would you rather...

*Be a famous actor **OR** a famous athlete?*

Would you rather...

*Only be awake at night **OR** during the day?*

Would you rather...

*Eat pizza for the rest of your life **OR** burgers?*

Would you rather...

*Only be able to eat breakfast **OR** dinner forever?*

Thank you for reading and Happy Easter to you and your loved ones!

CPSIA information can be obtained
at www.ICGtesting.com
Printed in the USA
LVHW081116060420
652355LV00018B/2167

9 781989 543962